LICENSE
TO SPEND

LICENSE TO SPEND

A retirement plan based on INcome as opposed to IFcome

Tim Whisler

CRPC®, CLTC®, Certified Financial Fiduciary®

Dedication

In memory of my mom Linda Whisler (1948-2000). You never saw one of my business cards, heard a podcast episode, or read a page from this book. But the memory of your love, support, and encouragement continues to fuel my passion to serve others. You are my inspiration for wanting to not just make a living but to make a difference. I look forward to our reunion in Heaven.

To my dad, Bill, thank you for your love, support, and encouragement throughout my life. I have so many wonderful childhood memories because of the love and sacrifice you shared with us. Your hard work taught me the importance of establishing a strong work ethic. Our family time together taught me the importance of making time for my family. Thank you for always asking how business is going and for our frequent lunches and golf rounds together. Thanks for being a part of my family and spending time with Cam and Cade. I love you, Dad!

To my sons Cam and Cade. I hope that you are relentless in your pursuit to find your passion and purpose in life. Give God the reins and let Him lead. He will bless you in ways we cannot explain or understand. You'll always be brothers and I hope you'll always be great friends. I'm so proud of you both and I love you very much. And yes, you qualify for a planning fee discount.

To my bride Ronda. I can only imagine what went through your mind back in 2004 when I said that I needed to leave corporate America and pursue self-employment as a business owner. The journey has certainly been bumpy, and I am sorry for those times. Thank you for listening to me as I share my excitement about a marketing idea and for your patience as I ask you for help with making certain decisions. Thank you for taking time out of your day to help me at educational workshops and client events. Thank you for your love, support, and all you do for our family. I love you very much!

CONTENTS

Introduction

According to a 2022 survey, 66% of Americans fear that they will run out of money in retirement.[1]

Are you one of them?

If you are, know that you're not alone—in my decades of helping people prepare for retirement, countless people have walked into my office with this same fear.

No one has taught you the ins and outs of retirement planning, and now that you're facing dozens of life-altering financial decisions, you feel overwhelmed and out of your depths.

These are some of the questions that make your head spin and keep you up at night:

---

[1] GOBankingRates. (n.d.-b). 66% of Americans are worried they'll run out of money in retirement — here are 7 tips to make sure that doesn't happen. *Nasdaq.* https://www.nasdaq.com/articles/66-of-americans-are-worried-theyll-run-out-of-money-in-retirement-here-are-7-tips-to-make

- How much money do I need to have saved before retirement?
- When should I turn on Social Security?
- What will happen if I face unexpected health expenses?
- Will my spouse be okay financially if I pass away first?
- How will taxes affect my retirement portfolio?

But on top of these fears, you have a dream...

As you worked for decades, you imagined your dream retirement. Through the good days and the bad, as you put in long hours and saved money, you dreamed of an ideal retirement future that would one day be yours.

This looks different for everyone. Maybe you want to travel everywhere you couldn't travel while you were working. Maybe you want to move closer to your grandkids and be there to support them as they grow up. Maybe you want to delve into a hobby, charity work, or small business idea.

The beauty of retirement is that your time is now your own. You can finally accomplish everything you couldn't during your career years.

But now, as retirement looms closer, you fear that your retirement dreams won't come true. You fear that you won't have the money to live the retirement life you want. You fear that you'll have to sacrifice the plans you've been daydreaming about for decades.

You don't have to live with this fear any longer.

Yes, I've seen countless people walk into my office with the same fears you're agonizing over now. But I've also seen these same people experience relief when they learn that they won't run out of money in retirement—and they can make their retirement dreams come true. I've watched these people walk out of my office excited for the future instead of dreading it.

The key is planning.

When you make your retirement plan, you will know for a fact that you will not run out of money in retirement. You'll know that you're financially prepared for any unexpected health costs. You'll know that your spouse and other family members will be provided for if you pass away. You'll be prepared to beat taxes and inflation.

And you'll know that you can make your dream retirement a reality...

As you approach retirement, you can let go of the sleepless nights and persistent worry.

You can embrace retirement as something to enjoy—not something to fear.

After your years in the workforce, don't you deserve to enjoy your retirement?

But your fears and worries won't disappear until you make your plan...

And the best way to fight fear is with knowledge.

In this book, I'm going to walk you through everything you need to know to move from retirement fear to retirement confidence.

Even if you know nothing about retirement, by the end of this book, you will be prepared to meet with an advisor and create your plan.

If you're ready to let go of your fears and build your dream retirement, read on...

CHAPTER 1

Can You Afford to Retire?

How much money will you need to have saved on the day you retire?

How will you know when you've saved enough?

Most people can't answer either of these questions.

The problem is, that there is no one-size-fits-all number that determines when a person has saved enough to retire. Retirement looks different for everyone.

To know how much money you need, the first step is figuring out what your ideal retirement looks like.

Are you looking to retire full-time or part-time? When you step away from your 40+ hour-a-week job, do you plan on pursuing a part-time job or an entrepreneurial endeavor? Will you bring in any income? Or do you want to pursue a full retirement—zero income but maximum time freedom? If you plan on making an income, that reduces the amount you'll need to save before retiring because you won't need to withdraw as much.

Do you want to travel? Traveling is one of the most common retirement dreams I hear from clients. But it's not enough to say you want to travel—make your vision more specific. How often do you want to travel? What kinds of trips do you want to take? Will you only travel domestically, or do you have international vacation plans? What destinations are on your must-see list? Are you picturing weekend RV trips to national parks or frequent stays in fancy hotels? Where do your kids, grandkids, and other relatives live? How often do you want to visit them?

What hobbies are you looking forward to enjoying? Will you need to buy any memberships or equipment to participate in those hobbies? Some hobbies are more expensive than others— restoring classic cars costs much more than knitting.

Take stock of what your ideal retirement looks like—it's a better indicator of how much you need to save for retirement than any number you hear on the news.

Do you have a "volatility buffer"?

Your ideal retirement isn't the only factor you need to consider...

Do you have enough saved to withstand the damage that market volatility can do?

What happens if the market crashes again?

You lived through 2000. You lived through 2008. You lived through 2022.

It will inevitably happen again...

And the longer you live, the more likely it is that you will see it happen.

Many people are not aware of the damage that market volatility will do to an income plan. The damage from market volatility can cause a person to not have enough money to live off of in retirement.

That's a scary place to be.

One thing I hear from people all the time is, "I can't afford a significant loss to my assets because I don't have time to recover."

When the market crashes, we know there's a chance it could recover eventually. But when you're retired, you might not live long enough or be able to hold off using that money long enough to wait for that time without losing all of your savings.

The market can remain irrational, longer than you can remain solvent.

You might encounter a "lost decade." Take a look at the image below. If you had invested $100,000 into the S&P 500 on January 1, 2000, your money was worth significantly less in January 2010. That's what we would call a lost decade. Can you imagine the feeling of drawing income while watching your account suffer losses? You could run out of money.

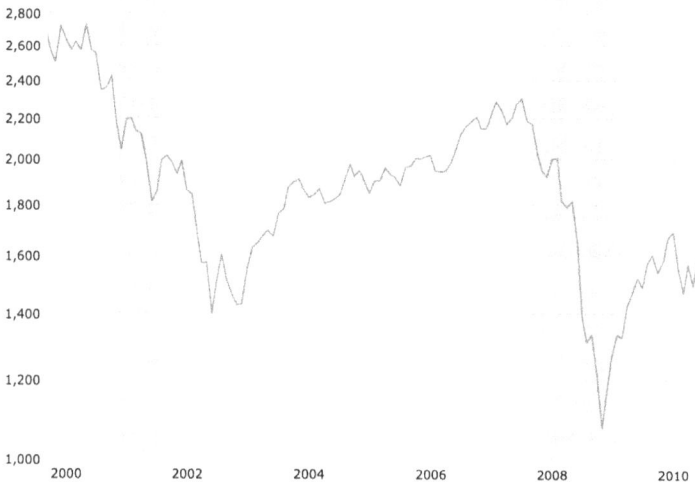

(Source: https://www.macrotrends.net/2324/sp-500-historical-chart-date)

When investments are catered towards average annual returns, they're only telling half the story. Remember, it's only the average. You might think something will be a good investment because the average annual return was 7% over the last ten years...But that number doesn't tell you that there will be some bad years and some good years. If you're relying on that investment to supply your income in retirement, you'll be in trouble when a bad year rolls around. During your working years, when you weren't taking money out of that investment, a bad year didn't impact your income. But now, your money may not recover from that loss.

Some people might read this and think, "Well, if I don't have my money in the market, the only other option is to cash it all in and stuff it underneath the mattress or bury it in the backyard." They don't know that there's an alternative out there.

Before you retire, you need to ensure you have a "volatility buffer." This is a bucket of money you can pull from when the market is bad. That way, you don't have to make withdrawals from any assets that are depreciating because of market volatility. You'll have somewhere else to pull income from.

Where will that money come from? Do you have that "buffer" yet?

The volatility buffer is critical—it's something I work with every one of my clients to create. And the volatility buffer is NOT about putting all of your money into cash.

We'll talk more about creating your volatility buffer in a later chapter, but for now, take a moment to assess whether you already have one or not. A bond fund is NOT a volatility buffer.

Will the Money You've Saved Last Long Enough?

The #1 retirement fear I hear from people is: "I don't want to outlive my money."

The fear of dying has been surpassed by the fear of outliving your money...

I understand why this terrifies people...

Imagine you're in your 90s and you run out of money after a few decades of retirement. You're too old to work; maybe you have health problems. What would you do?

This fear plagues even people who have millions of dollars.

Most people, even the wealthy, have no idea how to gauge when they've saved "enough."

Why? People have a (sometimes debilitating) fear of the unknown.

You only retire once in your life, so you can't "practice" retiring. When it comes time for you to retire, you suddenly have to make life-altering decisions you've never made before. You won't know what the retirement process looks like until you're in it. This can feel overwhelming for many people. All of the unknowns cause stress, and people throw up their hands and say, "I'm not ready. I haven't saved enough."

Fear will lead to what retirement expert Tom Hegna calls a "Just in Case retirement." Many people get into a mindset of saving everything "just in case," but never spending it. They save money for a new boat, but then they never spend the money on the boat—"just in case" they need the money later. They're always too scared to spend that money. Eventually, these people die without spending the money, and then who gets the boat? Their kids.

The "just in case" retirement happens when people let fear of the unknown rule them. They don't know how much money they need in retirement, so they start hoarding money with no plan.

But how do we beat the fear of the unknown? We make the unknown known.

We're going to put together a plan that gives you a license to spend. You're going to know once and for all when you have saved enough to retire. That way, you can spend that money you've worked so hard to earn—while knowing you have safeguards in place to provide for you in retirement. We're going to take away your fear of the unknown and give you the ability to enjoy your retirement.

Retirement isn't all about saving, it's about spending, too. You've worked hard all your life, so retirement should be the phase of life when you get to enjoy the rewards of your work. Buy the boat. Take the vacation. But because most people are afraid of running out of money, the only way to ensure you have peace of mind when spending your money is to create a plan. If you don't have a plan, you'll end up with a "just in case" retirement.

Answering the question "Have I saved enough?" will ease your anxiety. There's too much marketing out there that says you need a certain dollar amount to have a comfortable retirement. That's a myth. It's completely false. The dollar amount you need depends on the lifestyle you want to live. Everyone will have a different amount because everyone has a different vision of a happy retirement.

On the opposite end of the "just in case" spectrum, I've had some frustrating experiences working with wealthy people who think they'll never run out of money. Some people think that as soon as they add that second comma to their account value, they're protected. But the more money you have, the more you want to spend. If you've grown accustomed to an expensive lifestyle, you're not going to want to cut back when you retire. Plus, higher withdrawals lead to higher taxes, which can erode wealth quickly. Even those who have millions of dollars in the bank need to plan for retirement—just having that huge pile of money isn't enough.

Having a big pile of money will do you no good if you don't have a plan for the lifestyle you want to lead. Just look at how many lottery winners or star athletes go broke. The dollars were there, but these people didn't understand how to manage them. But if you can say, "These are the things I want to do in retirement. This is how much everything will cost," you might find that you don't need as big a pile of money as thought to achieve a retirement that will make you happy.

That's why it's critical to step back and decide what kind of retirement you want. Being on a cruise every month will cost more than staying local and volunteering, but which version of retirement is fulfilling to you? If your expectations exceed what you can afford, we'll rein them in, but you need to get clear on what your ideal looks like so we can plan to get you as close to it as possible.

An Investment In Knowledge...

In one of my previous offices, I had one of my favorite Benjamin Franklin quotes on the wall: "An investment in knowledge pays the best interest." I wanted everyone who walked into that office to understand that it's okay not to know things—but it's a huge mistake to remain ignorant. It's normal to not understand much about retirement. But when you recognize that you lack this knowledge, it's your responsibility to seek out someone who can fill in the gaps for you. Many times, I'll get clients with what I call "peacock personality." These people were successful in their chosen industry and are probably used to being the smartest person in the room. But they know next to nothing about retirement. I try to help these people understand that it's perfectly okay. They're not any less intelligent because they lack experience in this area. But if they let pride get the best of them and try to do this planning alone, they could be sabotaging their retirement without even realizing it.

The good news is that very few plans I see are wrong, most are just incomplete. When I sit down with a new client, I never have to say, "No, you're never going to retire. This is a mess." As long as you have something saved, you're on your way. My job is then to finish what you've started. "Okay, you have some savings. How are we going to protect them? How are we going to withdraw it without the IRS taking more of it?"

> **Deaccumulation is the most complex part of retirement."**
>
> Dr. William Sharpe

You've made your money, but now that you need to use it in retirement, there are a lot of moving parts. You may not understand all these moving parts yet, but that's okay. This might be your first time planning a retirement, but I've planned thousands. I'm here to help you understand some of the most important decisions you'll need to make...

CHAPTER 2

Your Tax Problem, the IRS, and The Stealth Tax

All the years you were working, you were taught to defer your taxes. You've done what you were told...and it's created a big tax bill. Now what? How will you ensure it doesn't consume your savings and keep you from enjoying the retirement you want?

A lot of people come to me with regret that they put too much into the tax-deferred bucket versus the tax-free bucket. I always try to ease their self-criticism by reminding them that they were doing what they were told to do.

When you're building a 401k, you're taught to contribute as much to it as you can because your company will match it. You were never taught that tax-free was better than tax-deferred. You were just taught to defer. Now you have a huge 401k—but it's not all yours.

And tax rates will increase over time...

Would you apply for a mortgage that said, "Today your rate is going to be X percent, but over the next 20 years, we're going to dictate what your rate is going to be"? Nobody would sign that. But that's what the IRS does. We've all followed what Wall Street told us to do: defer the taxes. But what happens when years pass, it's time to pay the taxes, and your rate is significantly higher?

Let's say you have a million-dollar 401k. You're 60 years old and you don't have to take money out for 13 years. Can you imagine what a million dollars could grow to in 13 years? If the value of that account doubles, by the time you start taking money out of it, you have $2 million. The rate you're taxed at will be much higher. We can plan around this and start taking out a portion each year, paying taxes on it at current income tax rates, and then taking the net result and putting it into a tax-free bucket.

A lot of people think they're going to be in a lower tax bracket in retirement because they're earning less. But they don't consider that they will still have a tax liability when they're receiving income from Social Security or qualified accounts.

And you have to worry about Required Minimum Distributions (RMDs) and Income Related Monthly Adjustment Amounts to Medicare Part B (IRMAA)...all combining to create your looming tax problem...

When you have funds inside a qualified account (which means it has never been taxed), at some point down the road, the government says you have to begin taking required minimum distributions. By this time, some people have already started to draw income off of a 401(k), 403(b), or traditional IRA. But many people have not because they have enough money coming in from Social Security and pensions. All of a sudden, they turn 73...The RMD says that in the year you turn 73, you have to begin taking a percentage of the value of the qualified account. This is how they calculate that percentage: on December 31 of the previous year, they will look at your account value and use a life expectancy table to determine your percentage. You must then take the first withdrawal by April 1st of the year following when your RMDs are set to begin.

Taking withdrawals from qualified accounts is different than taking withdrawals from a 401k. You can't combine the value of the 401k and the value of the traditional IRA to fulfill your RMD.

If someone has already turned on income, the income they are withdrawing will count towards the RMD, which may fulfill the RMD requirement for that year. We make sure our clients are meeting their RMD requirements each year.

If you have a certain amount of money coming in, the government will tax up to 85% of your Social Security benefit.

Your income also determines what your Medicare Part B premium will be.

To make things worse, there will undoubtedly be future legislation that could disrupt your retirement plan. As I'm writing this book, the SECURE Act 2.0, which modified the RMD ages, was just passed. The Constitution was written in ink, but the IRS uses pencil. The laws you're basing your decisions on today could look different in the years ahead. This is what we call "legislative risk."

Your Silent Partner

Your silent retirement partner is...the IRS.

The IRS has an interest in nearly every asset you own.

Most of the time, you will be taxed on withdrawal, and how much you're taxed depends on which type of asset you own.

The money you have in your qualified accounts, such as your traditional IRA, is going to be taxed at your current income rate, which is generally the highest rate that anyone would ever pay.

If you have money in a Roth account, you've already paid the taxes on those funds.

If you have money in real estate or investments that aren't within an IRA, other tax rates will apply.

If it's non-qualified money, there's a cost basis involved. Your principal has already been taxed, but any gain from that investment will realize a short-term or long-term capital gain. If it's tax-deferred, there's going to be a tax liability that's due whenever you take a withdrawal from it. Your income tax liability can vary from year to year based on withdrawals.

The tax trap of inherited IRAs

When an IRA owner passes away, the IRS doesn't die... If a retired husband and wife have an IRA and one spouse passes away, the other spouse can take over ownership of the IRA. But when there's a non-spouse beneficiary such as a child or other relative, the beneficiary will have to pay taxes on the IRA. If you have an inherited IRA, when you withdraw from it, it'll boost your taxable income, causing you to pay taxes you hadn't expected.

The Stealth Tax

Inflation is the time bomb that destroys retirement plans. It's a "stealth tax" that reduces your purchasing power…and many people aren't prepared for it.

Have you heard of the Rule of 72? If we have a certain inflation rate (let's use 3% for our example), and it continues consistently for X number of years, 72 divided by the percentage of inflation will result in the number of years in which your money is worth half as much as it is the current year. 72 divided by 3 is 24, so in 24 years, your money would be worth half as much.

Imagine you plan to spend $5,000 a month in retirement. Today, $5,000 might be able to buy everything you want and need, but what happens in 30 years?

In 1991, a pound of coffee[2] cost $2.81. In 2021, a pound of coffee cost $4.71 (US Inflation Calculator, 2024a).

In 1991, a dozen eggs cost $0.99. In 2021, a dozen eggs cost $1.67 (US Inflation Calculator, 2024e).

---

[2] US Inflation Calculator. (2024a, April 10). *Coffee Prices Adjusted for inflation | US Inflation Calculator.* US Inflation Calculator | Easily Calculate How the Buying Power of the U.S. Dollar Has Changed From 1913 to 2023. Get Inflation Rates and U.S. Inflation News. https://www.usinflationcalculator.com/inflation/coffee-prices-by-year-and-adjust-for-inflation/

In 1991, a gallon of gasoline cost $1.20. In 2021, a gallon of gasoline[3] cost $3.13.

The cost of a Thanksgiving dinner was $32.37 in 2000 and $64.05 in 2022.[4] If you haven't planned for inflation, what will you do in twenty years when the price has risen even higher? Who aren't you inviting? Are you cutting the cranberry sauce or the sweet potatoes?

If a client tells me they want to put $300 a month aside for a future car payment on a new truck, I'll stop and ask them how many years into the future they're planning on buying this truck. $300 won't be worth the same in five years. You need to take inflation into account when you plan for the purchases you want to make in retirement.

If you plan to travel in retirement, you may not think about the fact that plane tickets will cost more in five years than they do today.

Inflation won't just affect your expenses. It'll affect your income, too. During your working years, your salary rose to meet

---

[3]   U.S. Bureau of Labor Statistics, Average Price: Gasoline, All Types (Cost per Gallon/3.785 Liters) in U.S. City Average, retrieved from FRED, Federal Reserve Bank of St. Louis, April 12, 2022

[4]   American Farm Bureau Federation. (n.d.). *American Farm Bureau Federation – Thanksgiving dinner cost survey.* https://www.fb.org/imgz/Year-Over-Year-Price-Comparison_2023-11-16-163225_oyma.pdf

inflation. Now, you'll need to ensure your income will beat inflation when you're withdrawing from assets in retirement.

Most pensions aren't adjusted for inflation. $1,200 a month today can buy more than it will be able to in ten years...Your dollar is stretched thinner over time.

The good news is, we can battle inflation with your retirement plan. Inflation doesn't mean that you'll have to spend less or make sacrifices as time goes on and your dollar is worth less.

CHAPTER 3

The Surviving Spouse Problem

You're gone...what can your spouse expect?

When one spouse dies, the other is left to bear all of the financial decisions and responsibilities of retirement alone.

I call this "the surviving spouse problem."

Usually, couples make financial decisions together. They use each other as a sounding board to make sure they're doing the right thing. All of a sudden, one of them is gone, and the surviving spouse has to make decisions alone.

In many couples I see, one spouse is primarily responsible for the couple's financial decisions. When I meet with couples, it's usually easy to tell which spouse is the "quarterback" when it comes to finances. What happens if that spouse dies first? The surviving spouse has let the other person take care of business for decades and now has to pick up the pieces and try to understand how to manage everything. Who will the surviving spouse turn to? Are there adult children or other relatives who can help? What resources does the surviving spouse have for making good financial decisions? Every couple needs a contingency plan in place so that if the "financial quarterback" of the pair passes away first, the surviving spouse will know what to do when their life is flipped upside down.

The surviving spouse is dealing with this financial burden during one of the most difficult periods in a person's life. Aside from finances, this person is now reconciling with spending the rest of retirement alone.

When both spouses were alive, they traveled together, visited the grandkids together, and did hobbies together. Now, the surviving spouse is alone. What will daily life look like? How will the surviving spouse adjust? How does your vision of the "ideal retirement" shift when you have to face life alone?

It's important to have purpose in life. When you were working, you had a built-in sense of purpose. Every day someone gave you goals and deadlines to accomplish. When you retire, you need a purpose to keep your mind and body active. It's easier to create a sense of purpose when you have someone to share your life with, but when your spouse passes away, it can be difficult to know what to do with yourself. You might be flooded with love and attention from friends and family when a death occurs, but at some point, the visitors go home and the meals from the church stop coming. Suddenly, the surviving spouse begins a new chapter of life alone.

Do you have a plan for what you would do if you become the surviving spouse? Does your spouse have a plan for what they would do if you passed away first? How will both of you find purpose in retirement if the other passes away?

This topic isn't pleasant to face, but the sad reality is that one spouse will pass away before the other. It's crucial to have a plan in place—for both finances and lifestyle—to minimize the surviving spouse's hardship.

The Social Security Death Cut

Do you know what happens to your Social Security payments when your spouse dies?

When one spouse passes away, the lower of the two benefits goes away.

Yes, that's right, when your spouse passes away, you lose one of the two Social Security benefits you shared as a couple.

For example, if a husband has a $3000 per month benefit and his wife has an $1800 per month benefit, and the husband passes away first...the wife would lose her $1800 per month benefit and take over her deceased husband's $3000 per month benefit.

With one benefit gone, we need to figure out how you can maintain the same standard of living as you did when your spouse was living. The wife in our example is now losing $21,600 a year in income that she would have received if her husband was still alive. How will she replace that? Where will that income come from?

This loss of income comes at the worst possible time. You're grieving...and you get a pay cut for your trouble. You're dealing with a difficult loss—you don't have time or energy to spend on stressing about your finances. This is the period of your life when it may feel comforting to keep everything in your life the same as it used to be before your loss...you don't want to be forced to make budget cuts or lifestyle changes when you're simply trying to figure out how to go on without the person you loved.

Tragedy catches most people off guard. There's never a good time for it. Losing your spouse is going to cause a tremendous upheaval in your life—the least you can do for yourself is minimize the financial burden by planning ahead. When the worst happens, you'll thank yourself for taking care of business years in advance so you can focus on what matters.

Many people assume that retirement will be cheaper after one spouse passes away because there's now only one person's living expenses, not two. You might have some cheaper living expenses, but you're now only living off of one person's income. You need to have a plan for where you're going to pull money from to replace this income.

The Surviving Spouse's Challenge

When a spouse dies, the surviving spouse is not only grappling with the grief of losing their life partner, but they must also make a myriad of decisions in a short time. It is estimated that the surviving spouse must make over 100 decisions related to the deceased's affairs within the first 48 hours after their death.

Imagine having to make significant and consequential decisions during possibly the worst, most emotionally difficult 48 hours of your life. How could you expect to get all of those 100+ decisions correct? At a time like that, you're emotionally spent and you likely won't be thinking logically. That's why planning is vital. The more you plan, the fewer decisions you'll have to make in that difficult moment. Planning is merely thinking and making decisions in advance.

The last thing you want to do is make huge financial decisions in the days after a death. Whether you're working with an advisor or not, do not make any important financial decisions during that time.

You're about to go through a dramatic life adjustment, and you don't want to make anything worse for yourself by making decisions when you're not in the clearest state of mind. Put a plan in place so you can give yourself time to grieve undisturbed.

Can you be at peace knowing your spouse will suffer?

John and Jane first met with me in 2016 after attending one of my Social Security seminars. In our Discovery Meeting, they shared information about their ideal retirement, their concerns, and the details of their assets. One of their first to-do items was to create a plan for an old 401(k) that John owned from employment at a previous job. They weren't planning on touching the funds from this account while they continued to work.

Their plans were to retire in about 4 years and, because these funds would play a key role in creating retirement income, they did not want to lose them to market volatility. The scars from losing thousands during the 2008 crisis were still pretty fresh.

After we had a couple of separate conversations and reviewed options, John liked the idea of moving the funds into a fixed-indexed annuity. The funds would be protected from market volatility and would have the opportunity to earn interest credits when the indexes would realize gains. So we completed the paperwork, rolled the 401(k) into the policy as a Traditional IRA, and the policy was soon issued. John and Jane would be well prepared when they wanted to retire in a few years.

Fast forward 8 months. John and Jane called the office and asked to see me immediately. Having experienced this type of call in the past from other clients, I feared that this was not good news. A few hours later, they arrived, and the looks on their faces confirmed the worst. John had just been diagnosed with pancreatic cancer. He vowed that he would do everything in his power to fight, but he wanted to put together a plan for Jane in case he would not be able to defeat this horrible disease.

My heart hurt for John and Jane as I could only imagine what they were now going through. We were able to only meet one more time as the treatments were taking such a toll on John's body and weakening him to the point where daily activity became a tremendous battle. But once John made that plan for Jane, the couple could let go of financial worries and focus on making John's last days as peaceful as possible. A few weeks later, John lost his battle with cancer and passed away at 66 years of age.

A couple of months after the funeral, Jane requested to have a meeting with me. Her son, daughter, and son-in-law came with her. We now needed to begin the process of executing the plan for Jane that we had created before John's passing. Jane wanted to keep working so she would remain busy and continue to have a purpose each day while grieving the loss of her husband. So our plan was to now create an income strategy for Jane so she could retire as soon as she was ready. We met several times over a period of about a year so I could share information in small pieces with Jane and her family. John had gladly handled the finances for him and Jane for years, so I wanted to be sure that we acclimated Jane to the world of finances at a pace that was comfortable for her.

About 18 months following John's passing, Jane officially retired. Implementing the income plan for Jane has included a strategic plan of her receiving Social Security from John's benefit which was paid to Jane as a widow benefit. As she received monthly income from John's benefit, this allowed her to defer her primary Social Security benefit which increased the payout by 8% each year of deferral until Jane turned 70. A few years later when she celebrated her 70th birthday, we switched over to her primary Social Security benefit which provided her with more monthly income than what she had been receiving from John's.

To complement the monthly benefit from Social Security, she has been receiving monthly income from an IRA account that we are managing for her. While this will continue to happen for a few more years, a larger IRA sitting inside of a fixed indexed annuity with a lifetime income rider is waiting on the sidelines. This policy will then provide her monthly income for the duration of her lifetime, even if the account value is depleted. Jane and her kids know that she will have the monthly income she needs to get her through retirement.

If Jane and John hadn't had that plan in place, Jane would've had to deal with so much more on top of her husband's tragic passing. During her last days with her husband, she would have also had to deal with the fear of "What am I going to do?"

During retirement planning sessions, I've seen so many wives break down in tears saying, "When he's gone, I don't know what I'm going to do." This is a real fear for many couples, especially when one partner isn't well-versed in the world of finances. But we can take that fear away today. You can make these decisions now, while your spouse is alive and sitting next to you.

CHAPTER 4

Uncovering Your Retirement Truth

Where are you now in your retirement timeline? Are you near retirement, in retirement, or a long way off from retirement?

Are you in "The Fragile Decade"? This is the 5 years before retirement through the five years after retirement. These ten years are critical to planning.

Where you are now is going to tell us what the game plan should be. Our action steps are going to look different if you want to retire in 5 years vs if retirement is still in the distant future.

As the saying goes, "Most people don't plan to fail, but many fail to plan." Once you know where you are on your retirement timeline, you can begin planning what your retirement will look like.

Your Ideal Retirement

It's your first day after retiring...what's your purpose now?

For 40+ years of your life, your career has provided you with a purpose from the moment you woke up each morning. You had a defined role and knew what tasks you needed to get done each day. What happens when that goes away? When you have your retirement party and pack up your office, what happens when you wake up the next Monday morning? How do you plan to spend your day? And the next day, and the next day, and the next...

Retirements without purpose fail, even when the money is there.

Having so much free time is one of the great blessings of retirement, but it can turn into a curse. Humans need a purpose for our physical and mental well-being. Sitting on the couch, eating snacks, and watching TV might be a fun change of pace the first week you don't have to go to work...but it'll get old fast. If you don't find meaningful ways to fill the time you used to spend at work, you'll be bored out of your mind.

Studies suggest that there is a correlation between early retirement and an earlier death. Why? Many people neglect their physical and mental health after they retire. Without a job to get them out of bed in the morning, provide them with a purpose, keep them active, and stimulate social interaction, many retirees begin to suffer from mental health issues. Physical health will decline if mental health isn't strong... I've seen it happen to many people. How will you maintain your mental and physical well-being in retirement? How will you find a purpose each day when you don't have a job?

What does your ideal retirement look like? What do you want to do? Who do you want to do it with? Where do you want to do it?

The most common retirement plans I hear from clients are: travel, volunteer, take up a hobby, and spend time with family. All of these things are great, but they're vague. I challenge people to make these dreams as specific as possible. Where do you want to travel? How often do you want to visit your kids? What specific hobbies or volunteer organizations are you excited to get involved with? The clearer your picture is, the easier it will be to ensure your finances will make it all possible. And aside from finances, taking the time to imagine your post-retirement life in detail will make the transition easier. If you have only vague plans to "travel," it'll be easy to end up watching TV on the couch for too long without doing any traveling. But if you have specific, concrete plans, you'll be excited and full of purpose when you wake up on that first post-retirement Monday morning.

Your retirement lifestyle isn't going to look the same forever. Think about it...if you retire in your 60s and live into your 90s, that's 30 years. Your health and energy will shift a lot over these years. That's why I encourage people to think of retirement as three phases: the fast lane, the slow lane, and the sidewalk.

> *Think of retirement as three phases: the fast lane, the slow lane, and the sidewalk.*

The fast lane is the first and youngest phase of retirement. Your health and energy will be at their highest. If you have any big travel plans or ambitious projects to tackle, this would be the time to do it. Financially, it makes sense for you to plan to spend more money here than in later years. You want to be able to enjoy your money while you have the energy to.

In the slow lane years, you'll have less energy, but you may still be somewhat active. Maybe you no longer feel up to international travel, but instead, you take more local trips to visit relatives. We'll make sure you still have money to enjoy, but you'll be naturally inclined to spend less as you age.

The sidewalk years are the oldest age of retirement. Here, you'll spend the least amount of money because you won't have the energy to do as much.

When you visualize your ideal retirement, it's important to consider how it'll change over these three phases.

I like to give my clients a "Dream Retirement Brainstorm List" to help them get ideas for what they want to do in retirement. Here are some of the ideas on that list:

- Take up a sport (ex: golf, tennis, swimming)
- Learn an instrument
- Take art classes
- Take your financial advisor to dinner ;)
- Start a board game group with friends
- Join a local volunteer group
- Take walks or bike rides around the neighborhood
- Get into photography
- Work on sewing or knitting projects
- Join a book club
- Learn a language
- Research your family tree
- Take cooking classes
- Visit national or state parks
- Host movie nights with friends/neighbors
- Get into DIY home improvement projects
- Fishing
- Attend sporting events
- Get a pilot's license
- Gardening
- Join a community theatre
- Learn mixology
- Start a business
- Go camping

If there's anything you've said you've "always wanted to do but never had the time," retirement is the time to do it. When we know what your retirement dreams are, we can ensure your finances support them...

The 3 Key Questions That Dictate Your Retirement Finances

1) **What assets do you have that can be used in retirement?**

   Are you still working? What's your gross salary? Do you project any raises in the years before you retire?

   What assets do you have? Most people have some combination of the following:

   - Bank accounts
   - 401K
   - Traditional IRA
   - Life insurance
   - Long term care policies
   - Social Security
   - Equity in your home
   - Defined benefit plan
   - Pension plan

- Roth IRA
- Investment accounts

2) How much income will you need every month?

Many people struggle to answer this question. When you were working, you had a paycheck come to you on a regular basis. Now, that's gone. Your job dictated what your income was. Now that you have control over it, it can be difficult to know how much is enough.

This is why painting the picture of your ideal retirement is so important. When you understand what you want your lifestyle to be, it becomes easier to break down the potential expenses involved.

3) How much risk are you comfortable with?

Just because you were risky when you were building your wealth, you do not need to be risky in this phase of life. In retirement, you still need growth, but you can achieve that without being risky. Wall Street has misled people into believing that growth requires risk, but that's a risk. (We'll cover this in detail in Chapter 6).

CHAPTER 5

What's Your Current Plan? (Everyone Has a Current Plan)

The most difficult retirement planning question is: how long do you see yourself in retirement?

The hidden question there is: How long do you expect to live?

This question is tough because:

a) Nobody likes to think about their own death
b) We will never know the answer (until it happens)

This is the paradox of retirement planning. We need to ensure you have enough income to last the rest of your life, but we will never know exactly how long you're going to live.

If retirement planning were easy, we'd know exactly when you were going to die, and we'd simply divide your income between the years you have left and drain the account with the last check going to the undertaker.

But we can't know how many years you have left. We don't have a crystal ball...

Of course, there are a few factors that might give us an idea. Do you have any known health problems? How long did your parents, grandparents, and siblings live? Did they have any health problems that you may inherit?

Even if we analyze these factors, death is unpredictable. We need to plan for the possibility that you'll live for a long time.

Today, we have more advanced medicine than ever before. It's not uncommon for people to live into their 90s. Even if not everyone lives that long, we need to plan as though you will so you won't outlive your money...

This means that, in most cases, there will be funds left over when you die. What do you want to do with those funds? What do you want your legacy plan to be? Do you want to set aside specific funds to leave to your kids and grandkids, or are they simply going to get whatever you haven't spent when you die? There are ways we can take action so your legacy gifts to your family aren't taxable. That way, you don't inadvertently make a legacy gift to the IRS...

Very few current plans are set up wrong, but many are incomplete. Many people have savings and assets, but they lack an income plan. An income plan mitigates the risks of market volatility, longevity, survivorship, taxes, inflation, and anything else that poses a significant threat to your retirement. If you've set up a plan either by yourself or with an advisor, what you have now is probably good, but now we need to take steps to preserve it. It's halftime of the game, and the second half determines if you win or lose.

Seeing your current plan visually

When your vision is clear, your decisions are easy.

When you see your current plan in an easy-to-read document, it's easy to assess where you're at on your retirement roadmap.

It's easier to understand where your risks, opportunities, and strengths are.

Having that plan in front of you will ease some of your anxiety. When all of the information is spread out across various spreadsheets and statements, it can be overwhelming to keep track of all the information.

But when you have that piece of paper in front of you, you don't have to wonder "Will I have enough money to live off of in retirement?" That piece of paper tells you. If there are gaps in your plan, now you know that your next step is to fill them. And if your plan is complete, that piece of paper is proof that you can stop worrying because everything will be okay.

Let me walk you through an example of how I might show a client their current plan...

First, the report will show the couple's Social Security start date (using full retirement age as a default) and gross monthly benefit. If the couple has any pensions, the report will show when those start and how much the monthly benefit will be, if the pension will increase with the cost of living, and if there are any survivability benefits.

Next, we look at an inventory of the couple's spendable assets. If the couple is still working, we can project what a 401(k) will grow to by retirement. Each asset is labeled with a tax classification, and this classification is very critical. We can also see how the assets are allocated: low-risk, at-risk, and emergency funds. The report will also show any protected assets such as real estate.

The couple will then fill out a risk assessment questionnaire. This will ask questions such as:

- What amount do you want in emergency funds?
- How many years will you let your assets grow before taking withdrawals?

- How do you feel about saving and risk?
- What would you consider reasonable interest or rate of return on your assets?

The report will then compare your current portfolio with your risk assessment. Here, the couple may see that their current portfolio is much more risky than their goals were in the assessment.

The report will show your current projected rate of return and monthly expenses. It will generate an itemized monthly budget with inflation factored in. It will show projected monthly cash flows and projected taxes.

The couple will then see a pre-retirement and post-retirement summary that shows their projected monthly income versus their projected monthly expenses for each year. This will highlight any cash flow problems with your current plan and show you when you will be drawing from spendable assets.

At some point in this yearly summary, there may be a red line. This line indicates when the couple would run out of money. If that red line appears too early...we have a problem.

But the good news is that this is just the current plan. The point of looking at this report is so we can see where we need to make changes. If we see that this couple's red line occurs too early, we can take action to push it down the page.

We can also input hypothetical death dates or long-term care dates. How will your spouse's red line change if you pass away a year into retirement? How will the red line change if you need long-term care at age 80?

Left Brain Vs Right Brain

There are two types of people: those who want to know how the clock is built and those who simply want to know what time it is. Some people will be content just seeing where the red line is and knowing "Will I be okay or do I need to make changes?" Other people will want to take the time to understand every moving part of the retirement report themselves. Both people are perfectly normal. If you're the "what time is it" person, you might feel overwhelmed when you look at the retirement report. The good news for you is, that as long as you're working with a retirement planner you trust, all you need to know is where that red line is. The rest can be taken care of for you. If you're the opposite type of person, a good retirement planner will be on board to help you understand your own finances. Different people have different learning styles, and we can ensure that no matter what type of brain you have, you can feel comfortable about your retirement. Even if you're not the "financial quarterback" of your family, we'll make sure you know what's going on.

Will your current plan support the lifestyle you want?

Now that you see your current plan, will it support your desired lifestyle?

If it does, fantastic. Our next step could be to create your legacy plan to distribute any leftover funds. Where do you want to have an impact in the world beyond your life?

If it doesn't, don't despair. Now is when we take action to improve it. We can move the red line down the page.

CHAPTER 6

The See-Saw Portfolio

Do you want your porfolio to dictate your lifestyle?

Or, would you rather be in control of your retirement lifestyle?

I ask every future client, "What does diversification mean to you?"

Most people answer something along the lines of: "Not having all your eggs in one basket. Having your investments set up so that if some are down, others are up, and I don't lose money."

Next, I'll ask, "Does diversification mean safety?"

Most people say no. They probably remember losing money in 2008 or they may have lost money in 2022.

Most investment vehicles offer two of these three elements: safety, growth, and liquidity.

When your investment has growth, it provides the opportunity for growth.

When your investment has safety, it's designed to protect the account value against loss.

When your investment has liquidity, you'll be able to take out money when you want to.

But in any investment, you can only have two of these three qualities.

CDs give you safety and liquidity but little growth—they pay a fixed rate of interest.

ETFs, stocks, and bonds give you growth and liquidity but without safety. Market losses can devastate account values.

Annuities give you safety and growth but reduced liquidity for a period of time.

Money markets give you safety and liquidity but may offer little growth.

You need a portfolio that covers the different types of investments—some with safety and liquidity, some with growth and liquidity, some with safety and growth.

> *A portfolio out of balance can cause issues with your retirement income.*

Different types of investments have different levels of risk. Usually, higher risk means a higher reward.

When introducing the importance of having a balanced portfolio for retirement income, we will review the characteristics of the three buckets that are broken down into pairs from Safety, Liquidity, and Growth.

The Conservative bucket provides Safety and Liquidity, but may be limited on Growth.

The Moderate bucket provides Safety and Growth, but may not offer full access to all of the funds.

The Aggressive bucket provides Growth and Liquidity, but may not provide Safety against loss.

A balanced portfolio will properly utilize the three buckets: Conservative, Moderate, and Aggressive.

For 40+ years, you've been taught that it's okay to take risk and chase yields. You've been told to leave money in the market when it's down and stay the course. When the market is up and you'd like to protect the gain you are asked, "why do you want to sell your winners?"

But when it comes to retirement, the kind of portfolio you've been taught to have is way too aggressive. If we leave too much in the aggressive bucket, your retirement plan is in harm's way. You have a "see saw" portfolio, and we need to balance it out.

On the other end of the spectrum, your portfolio might be too safe. You've been terrified of the market, but if you continue to play it overly safe you won't have enough growth to beat inflation.

The moderate bucket is where we're going to generate a lot of income because it has safety, but it also has growth potential.

The Illusion of Diversification

Diversification is supposed to keep you from losing money.

Unfortunately for many people, Wall Street has made up its own version of diversification.

And if you follow Wall Street's lead, you (like many before you) will lose a lot of money...

In this false version of diversification, when you're getting close to retirement, you would reallocate your holdings to something like 60% in stocks and 40% in bonds.

Let me remind you: In 2022, one of the most popular bond funds was down nearly 16%.

If you get "sold" Wall Street's version of diversification, your portfolio will be way too aggressive. The "conservative" elements of the Wall Street portfolio are just an illusion. You'll lose the money you need to live on in retirement.

Wall Street has an ulterior motive. When there's more money in the managed account, the advisor gets paid. They want everyone to have an aggressive portfolio so they can make as much money as possible. But when you're preparing to retire, you can't afford to buy into Wall Street myths. You need a truly diverse portfolio that balances safety and aggression so your future is protected.

Some years ago, I was invited to an interview by a local investment firm in central Illinois. I was honored by the invitation and went in for the interview. During the meeting, I asked what I thought was a routine question: "How do you protect your clients from the down markets?"

Everyone in the room looked at me, confused. "What do you mean?"

I tried again. "When the markets are down and clients are taking income, how do you protect the integrity of that account so they don't lose money? Do you use indexed annuities?"

"We don't use those here," the interviewer said.

That is when I brought the conversation to an end because I was not a good fit with their firm. In retirement, there has to be an element of safety in a portfolio—you need to have a volatility buffer. Owning a retirement income plan that is based purely in the stock market is a dangerous game to play. If you encounter someone trying to sell you on one of these plans—run.

The Balanced Portfolio

Retirement is all about income. A balanced portfolio ensures you have enough income to live on without the risk that you'll lose it.

A balanced portfolio isn't so much about what assets you have, but where they are. Are your assets in under-performing funds? Are they overexposed to volatility?

In a balanced portfolio, that "see saw" isn't leaning too far to either conservative or aggressive. The portfolio will have a calculated amount of your funds properly allocated among the Conservative, the Moderate, and the Aggressive buckets. When the market becomes volatile, your portfolio has been prepared for this event. You will still have a retirement income plan designed to complement your Social Security payouts and pensions.

Take a look at this illustration of a mountain.

Climbing and descending a mountain is similar to the two phases of your financial life. The Accumulation Phase, your working years, is like climbing a mountain. When you reach retirement (the peak of the mountain), you now transition to the Distribution Phase which is like descending the mountain.

> *80% of mountain climbing accidents occur while going down the mountain. In the same way, most financial mistakes happen in the distribution phase.*

When you're in the accumulation phase, you're making your way up the mountain, looking forward to reaching the peak and transitioning into full-time retirement. The biggest challenge during this phase of your life is simply saving enough for retirement. During this phase you're working in your career, possibly paying off college loans, getting married, buying your first house, having kids...When you're raising your kids you're possibly more focused on saving for college tuition than saving for retirement, which seems far off into the distance. But one day, you reach the top of the mountain and realize you're ready for the next chapter of life...retirement and the distribution phase.

The act of retirement is simple—you just stop working. But the process of retirement is complicated. Now, you must create income from the assets you spent decades saving.

If you're like most people. Your portfolio is comprised of a variety of accounts, such as 401(k)s, 403(b)s, traditional IRAs, Roth IRAs, jointly-owned investment accounts, maybe an HSA account, and your bank accounts. The common denominator is that these accounts are made up of dollars, but that's where the similarity ends. When funds are withdrawn from these accounts, the tax event that occurs can vary between capital gains, income tax rate, or tax free. If we're dealing with an inherited account, we could be dealing with cost basis.

During our working years, we're concerned with the ROI you're probably already aware of: Return on Investment. But in our retirement years, the key factor to successfully navigating the distribution phase is to focus on a different ROI: Reliability of Income.

Retirement is all about income. To enjoy your ideal retirement, you're going to need income. Most people will have income from Social Security and maybe a pension. If you need more income than what those sources provide, you have to take distributions from your assets: hence the term Distribution Phase.

During this phase, you're going to be exposed to challenges that weren't an issue during the Accumulation Phase. Many people remember the pain that the dot-com collapse in 2000 caused them as they saw tens of thousands of dollars wiped away from their accounts. Then, just a few years later, the mortgage bubble burst, causing the 2008 financial crisis which, again, wiped away huge percentages of retirement account values. Recently, we just experienced another bear market in 2022 when the S&P 500 closed the year with a 19% loss. Unfortunately, you'll experience future bear markets during your retirement years. But despite the fact that you're no stranger to market volatility, there is a new wrinkle when market volatility occurs during the Distribution Phase. This new wrinkle is called Sequence of Returns risk, which we'll cover in detail in the next chapter. This is perhaps one of the most significant of all risks because of the damage it can cause to the value of your assets.

Other risks that await retirees are taxes, inflation, long-term care expenses, survivorship following the loss of a spouse, and longevity. The risk of longevity is the multiplier of all risks because the longer you live, the greater your chances of having to deal with all the other challenges.

The vehicle you used to build your wealth (aggressive investments) is not the right vehicle to beat the challenges that occur when you distribute your wealth. When you're in accumulation, you're okay with risk because you have time to rebuild if you lose money. But if you lose money while in distribution, you're relying on that money as your source of income—and you don't have time to rebuild.

In retirement, keep this in mind, it's not how much you earn—it's how much you keep.

A balanced portfolio will protect you so you can go down the mountain with less risk of a significant crisis.

CHAPTER 7

Spending Your Money in Retirement

In retirement, the ROI you have to worry about isn't Return On Investment...

It's Reliability of Income.

Once you retire, you need reliable streams of income. You can't just take distributions from an asset on a random basis. There have to be some guarantees involved.

When you have that balanced portfolio, the next step is to create income from your assets in the most tax-efficient manner. We need to figure out the withdrawal strategy that makes the most sense for you without giving too much to the IRS.

Your retirement is going to fail or succeed based on your ability to have constant streams of income. Since we don't know how long you're going to live, we need to make sure you don't end up with more days than money. To achieve this, we need safety measures in place to protect your assets—even for people who have a second comma in their portfolio.

The common denominator between volatility, taxes, and inflation is that these challenges will impact your income. Income is what will enable you to have the retirement lifestyle you want. You need reliable streams of income so these challenges don't impact your ability to have the lifestyle you want.

Some advisors today are still preaching the 4% withdrawal rate rule that was created back in the 90s. I feel sorry for the clients who buy into that because it's not a sustainable metric anymore. The 4% rule is the idea that if you modify your holdings to a 60/40 portfolio between stocks and bonds and only withdraw 4% of your starting account balance, you should have enough income to last you for 30 years. When interest rates start going down, the most recent studies said that if you're going to follow that rule, you should only take 2.8% if you want the income to last 30 years. Notice the word if. That's IFcome. I don't think anyone should retire with IFcome...

IFcome vs INcome?

Do you have IFcome or INcome? Is your plan based on "if this" and "if that"? Is your plan only reliable IF certain events occur, or is it 100% reliable no matter what? Who wants to live an "if" lifestyle? You deserve to live a peaceful, relaxing retirement knowing you WILL have income regardless of any "ifs."

Sequence of Returns

Let's look at an example of two investors, Jim and Pete during their Accumulation Phase. They each invested the same amount of money into the market and didn't withdraw a penny. They could each have different returns each year but will end up with the same amount of money after 20 years. Take a look at the chart on the next page.

Accumulation Phase

Jim			Pete		
Year	Return	Account Value	Year	Return	Account Value
0		$500,000	0		$500,000
1	28.88%	$644,400	1	-10.14%	$449,300
2	-6.24%	$604,189	2	-13.04%	$390,711
3	19.42%	$721,523	3	-23.37%	$299,402
4	9.54%	$790,356	4	26.38%	$378,384
5	-0.73%	$784,587	5	8.99%	$412,401
6	11.39%	$873,951	6	3.00%	$424,773
7	29.60%	$1,132,641	7	13.62%	$482,627
8	13.41%	$1,284,528	8	3.53%	$499,664
9	0.00%	$1,284,528	9	-38.00%	$309,792
10	12.78%	$1,448,690	10	23.45%	$382,438
11	23.45%	$1,788,408	11	12.78%	$431,313
12	-38.00%	$1,108,813	12	0.00%	$431,313
13	3.53%	$1,147,954	13	13.41%	$489,152
14	13.62%	$1,304,306	14	29.60%	$633,942
15	3.00%	$1,343,435	15	11.39%	$706,148
16	8.99%	$1,464,210	16	-0.73%	$700,993
17	26.38%	$1,850,468	17	9.54%	$767,867
18	-23.37%	$1,418,014	18	19.42%	$916,987
19	-13.04%	$1,233,105	19	-6.24%	$859,767
20	-10.14%	$1,108,068	20	28.88%	$1,108,068
Years 1-3 Return:		42.06%	Years 1-3 Return:		-46.55%
Avg. Annual Return:		5.62%	Avg. Annual Return:		5.62%

For illustration purposes only. These returns depicted are hypothetical and do not represent the actual accounts of any investors.

Notice the annual performance of Jim's investments and compare it to the annual performance of Pete's investments. The order of the investment performance for Jim's account was simply reversed for Pete. Jim's first 3 years are Pete's last 3 years. Both account values end up being the exact same after 20 years despite the sequence of returns. This is because neither Jim nor Pete took any withdrawals from their accounts during these 20 years.

But in retirement, you will need to make withdrawals from your investments each year because you need income. When withdrawals come into play, the sequence of returns could cause one investor to run out of money while the other investor doesn't. Notice below that Jim and Pete are now each withdrawing $25,000 per year.

Income Phase

Year	Jim Withdrawal	Return	Account Value	Year	Pete Withdrawal	Return	Account Value
0			$500,000	0			$500,000
1	$25,000	28.88%	$612,180	1	$25,000	-10.14%	$426,835
2	$25,000	-6.24%	$550,540	2	$25,000	-13.04%	$349,436
3	$25,000	19.42%	$627,600	3	$25,000	-23.37%	$248,615
4	$25,000	9.54%	$660,088	4	$25,000	26.38%	$282,605
5	$25,000	-0.73%	$630,452	5	$25,000	8.99%	$280,763
6	$25,000	11.39%	$674,413	6	$25,000	3.00%	$263,436
7	$25,000	29.60%	$841,639	7	$25,000	13.62%	$270,911
8	$25,000	13.41%	$926,150	8	$25,000	3.53%	$254,592
9	$25,000	0.00%	$901,150	9	$25,000	-38.00%	$142,347
10	$25,000	12.78%	$988,122	10	$25,000	23.45%	$144,865
11	$25,000	23.45%	$1,188,974	11	$25,000	12.78%	$135,184
12	$25,000	-38.00%	$721,664	12	$25,000	0.00%	$110,184
13	$25,000	3.53%	$721,256	13	$25,000	13.41%	$96,607
14	$25,000	13.62%	$791,086	14	$25,000	29.60%	$92,802
15	$25,000	3.00%	$789,069	15	$25,000	11.39%	$75,525
16	$25,000	8.99%	$832,759	16	$25,000	-0.73%	$50,156
17	$25,000	26.38%	$1,020,845	17	$25,000	9.54%	$27,556
18	$25,000	-23.37%	$763,116	18	$25,000	19.42%	$3,053
19	$25,000	-13.04%	$641,866	19	$25,000	-6.24%	$0
20	$25,000	10.14%	$554,316	20	$25,000	28.88%	$0
	Years 1-3 Return:	42.06%			Years 1-3 Return:	-46.55%	
	Average Annual Return:	5.62%			Average Annual Return:	5.62%	

For illustration purposes only. These returns depicted are hypothetical and do not represent the actual accounts of any investors.

The index performance is the same as during the Accumulation Phase but look at the end result and the difference between the two account values. Pete ran completely out of money in 18 years while Jim has more in his account than when he started. The reason? The sequence of the returns caused Pete to run out of money because his first three years of withdrawals occurred during market volatility. The significance of the volatility caused Pete to completely exhaust his account value. Despite the average annual return being equal for both investors, the sequence of the returns had a significantly different impact on their account values. Go back and look at the chart again because understanding this could prevent you from running out of money in retirement.

Many retirees reside in the same position as Pete but don't know it until it's too late. The advice that they received or their decisions as self-guided retirees was focused on selecting investments based on average rates of return. If you have an investment with an average return of 6%, that doesn't mean that every year will generate a 6% return. What happens to your account value when you have a return of 1% or a negative 18% and you're depending on that money for your income in retirement? Even worse, what happens to your account value if another 2008 or 2022 occurs while you're taking money from your accounts?

In our example with Jim and Pete, the average rate of returns was the same, but one investor ran out of money. A retirement plan based on an average rate of returns is the epitome of "IFcome." IF the market doesn't have a bad year, IF the average rate of return is x%, and if you don't withdraw more than planned, and so on. Do you see the problem?

Unfortunately, many many retirees' income plans are based upon IFcome.

A retirement plan based on an average rate of returns is the epitome of "IFcome."

In retirement, we need to be strategic about taking withdrawals from our assets. If an account is exposed to volatility, should you take a withdrawal at that time? Look back at what happened to Pete. This is why having a balanced portfolio is so important. An ideal retirement strategy involves multiple buckets of money with each bucket having a purpose for the funds. During volatile years, you can withdraw funds from the SAFE bucket. During growth years, you can pull from your GROWTH bucket. That way, you won't be reliant on a risky investment that may vary greatly in its returns year by year. As you may have a portion of your assets in risky investments because you want growth, you'll also want to have a separate portion that is safe so that when those risky investments are down, you don't have to withdraw from them and lock in your losses. You'll have another bucket to withdraw from that isn't subject to volatility.

But what happens when there aren't multiple assets to pick from? A retiree might just have a 401(k), a small Roth IRA, and Social Security. If you fall into this category, that's okay. We're going to incorporate the volatility buffer into your plan to protect against sequence of returns risk. We will find the right solution that is in your best interest to help protect your account value while also creating as much income as possible.

How Taxes Impact Your Retirement Income

You don't have one big pile of "retirement money." It's in different buckets. These different buckets will be taxed differently.

The tax classification of your funds (taxable, tax-deferred, tax-free) will dictate the role of the IRS when you make withdrawals. We need to factor this into your income strategy so that when you make a withdrawal, we'll know how much you actually get to keep. You need a withdrawal strategy to mitigate tax liability. This strategy will tell us which assets to pull from first to minimize your taxes.

Your CPA is just trying to save you taxes on a yearly basis, so the recommendation may be to defer. But when it comes time to take income in retirement, you'll have to pay taxes on what you've deferred.

Ed Slott has a famous line: "I'm a 40-year recovering CPA." He said that CPAs were teaching people the wrong way to handle taxes. CPAs were looking at taxes on a micro level rather than a macro level. They were trying to save taxes on a year-by-year basis but setting clients up for a huge tax bill in retirement. Now, he advises people that the best time to pay taxes is when they're at their lowest rates.

When people don't have a withdrawal strategy, they will jeopardize their ability to mitigate tax liability.

For example, I've had a client say, "Hey, I have this Roth account, but I also have this tax-deferred IRA account. I needed to do something so I pulled from my Roth IRA because I didn't want to pay taxes on the other one." What's the problem here? This client thought that pulling from the Roth would minimize their taxes. But by leaving money in the tax-deferred account, he's giving it the opportunity to grow. As the money in that account grows, so do the taxes.

Without a withdrawal strategy, you will probably pay more in taxes than you should have at the end of the day.

How Inflation Impacts Your Retirement Lifestyle

The #1 way to hedge against inflation is to protect as much of your assets as you can from volatility.

Once we've done that, either with indexed annuities, CDs, or anything else that has an element of safety, each time we withdraw, we have to ask if the withdrawal is going to keep you current with inflation.

Social Security will—it has a cost of living adjustment. Your pension may or may not have a cost of living adjustment.

One of the ways that we hedge against inflation is to use tools such as an indexed annuity. In the press, annuities often get a bad rep. But they have some unique advantages. One advantage of an indexed annuity is that you're able to capture the growth of market indexes such as the S&P 500. But you are protected against losses. When the index goes up, you have the opportunity for interest to be credited to your account value. When the index goes down, your account value is protected and you don't lose a penny.

There are 4 types of annuities: fixed, immediate, variable, and indexed.

Fixed: the interest rate is set by the insurance company and is guaranteed for a specific number of years.

Immediate: a lump sum value is sent to the insurance company which is converted to a specific amount to be paid back to the owner.

Variable: the account value is invested in sub-accounts (securities in the market) which can result in the account value rising and falling from the performance of the sub-accounts. The policy also includes many fees, including fees for the sub-accounts.

Indexed: the account value is protected from volatility and can earn interest from positive index performance. Interest can be credited from positive index performance via a cap rate, participation rate, or a spread. The base policy typically has no fees.

When you don't have enough assets to pull from, an indexed annuity is a possible solution. Not only will it protect the account value from market volatility, but there are indexed annuities that offer an income rider to provide lifetime income. Some companies offer an income rider that can increase the payout amounts which can help provide a hedge against inflation.

I usually explain income riders using the example of a home insurance policy. Your base home insurance policy may not cover specialty concerns such as a sewer drain in a basement or a large amount of jewelry. To provide coverage for such items, you add an extra rider to the policy. An indexed annuity gives you the opportunity for growth but protects you from the downside. With an indexed annuity that includes an income rider, the policy will provide income that you will never outlive and possibly give you an increasing payout over time.

If you do have enough assets to draw from, your hedge against inflation is having more money than you need today. Your goal will be to create growth while also having safety.

CHAPTER 8

Tax-Free Income in Retirement

Your silent retirement partner is...the IRS.

How much of your retirement income would you like to give to the IRS?

Zero, right?

Our good old friends at the IRS are always there to put their hands in your pockets. We're going to do everything we can to minimize how much of your income you'll need to hand over.

You did a great job saving money over the last few decades, but now, every time you withdraw that money to use as income, you're going to have to pay taxes on it to the IRS.

If someone has a million dollars in a 401K, they're not going to be able to take a million dollars out and keep it. Some of that will be taxed.

The four different ways the IRS will be looking to take money from you are:

1) RMDs (taxed at current income tax rates)
2) Social Security (up to 85% of your benefit can be taxed)
3) IRMAA/Medicare
4) Inherited IRAs (stretch IRAs are gone)

If a couple has already taken their RMDs, then passes it to their children after death, the children need to continue to take the RMDs each year. On top of that, the account needs to be liquidated within 10 years. If the kids are making $89K a year and are just on the threshold of a higher tax bracket, and then all of a sudden they inherit money, now they're pushed into that higher tax bracket. We want to avoid these kinds of tax issues for your beneficiary.

If a parent passes away younger than an RMD age, their beneficiary doesn't have to take any RMDs out per year, but the account still needs to be liquidated within ten years.

If the RMDs aren't taken out like they're supposed to, your heirs may be subject to a penalty from the IRS.

The Three Tax Buckets

Our money is broken down into three different tax buckets:

1) Taxable
2) Tax Deferred
3) Tax Free

In the taxable bucket, you're going to be taxed at a capital gains basis. There will either be short term or long term capital gains. An example of a taxable asset would be a non-qualified account such as a joint savings account shared between husband and wife. The cost basis would determine how much of a tax liability there would be when it comes time to take withdrawals. If a couple sets up a $50,000 account, and now that account is worth $75,000, the $25,000 gain would be the only amount taxable when the couple takes income from the account. Since the $50,000 they've put into the account over the years came from their working income, they've already paid income taxes on it. It doesn't need to be taxed a second time. But the $25,000 in gains is now taxable at a capital gains rate.

One of my clients inherited her father's non-qualified account when he passed away. Under the current laws, she has a stepped-up cost basis. It means that her taxable cost basis was calculated based on what the value of the asset was the day her father passed away. She won't get taxed on what her father put into it.

A tax deferred account is funded with pre-tax dollars. The tax deferred bucket includes traditional IRAs, 401(k)s, and 403(b)s. Since these accounts are funded with pre-tax dollars, you won't be taxed when you put money in, but you'll be taxed when you withdraw the money in retirement. This withdrawal will create a tax liability that is determined by your current income tax bracket. With a traditional IRA, you are not taxed on capital gains, you are taxed at regular income tax rates. Because it is a tax-deferred account, you don't pay taxes at the time you make the investment.

When you make a withdraw, you will pay taxes at your current income rate based on the amount of the withdrawal.

There will also be an RMD due on the tax deferred account. As of the date of writing, your RMD age depends upon your year of birth. If you were born in 1950 or earlier, you are already taking your RMDs. If you were born between 1951 and 1959, your RMD age is 73. If you were born in 1960 and later, your RMD age is 75.

One of the most common tax free accounts is the Roth IRA. It is funded with after-tax dollars. There are restrictions and rules to be followed when it comes to Roth IRA contributions. You also have the opportunity to convert funds from the tax-deferred account into a Roth, but again, there are rules and guidelines to follow.

Unlike the tax deferred account, there is no RMD due on a Roth IRA.

Your Withdrawal Strategy

Your withdrawal strategy is to move as much income to the tax free bucket as possible. This isn't possible in every situation, but it's worth looking into. When you take a withdrawal from a tax free bucket, you keep every penny. This is how you can offset inflation.

Two common tax free income buckets are Roth IRAs and life insurance.

When you have a Roth IRA, you can access funds without the IRS being involved. Does a Roth conversion make sense for you? One of the benefits of the Roth IRA is that you don't have to take RMDs. But if you don't think you're going to live much longer, it doesn't make sense to do this because you may not have time to reap the tax free benefits.

If we have time and you're in good health, however, we can build a tax free bucket with the benefits of a permanent life insurance policy. This is a fantastic vehicle to build tax free income and a tax free legacy.

This is the way I explain life insurance to clients: you can either own or rent a house. Either way, you have a roof over your head. When you're a renter, none of the maintenance is your responsibility, but when you leave that house, you have nothing to show for it, either. Meanwhile, the owner bears responsibility for the house. They pay real estate taxes and pay for repairs. The reward of doing so is that they build equity in that property. When they want to sell the house down the line, they'll be able to sell it for more than they purchased it for.

Life insurance works the same way. You can rent it or own it. When you pass away, it provides your family peace of mind.

Life insurance is the ultimate love letter. There is no greater way to show you care about the people in your life than ensuring that they'll be provided for should you die.

> *Life insurance is the ultimate love letter.*

Life insurance doesn't just have to have a death benefit, it can have a living benefit. With permanent life insurance, we like to utilize the indexed universal life policy, which is similar to an indexed annuity. In other words, it's not just paying out a flat fixed rate of return. The account value can appreciate based upon positive index performance. But the value of the account won't go down when there's a negative index. It'll just receive a zero. As time goes on and premiums are put into the policy, or as the index performance is positive, it creates an increase in the account value of the policy down the road. As the account value has appreciated over time, you can now borrow against the value of the account. You don't have to pay taxes on that, similar to what happens when someone takes out a home equity line of credit.

When I set this up for clients, our strategy is to fund it for a certain period of time, then turn off the premiums. But while those funds are still there, building growth based upon index performance, that account value will increase. Now, we can start taking withdrawals from that in the form of a "loan." You're taking out "loans" against the value of the contract. When you pass away, the loan is paid back to the insurance company, so the death benefit is reduced by the value of the loan. When the policyholder dies, the policy proceeds, net of the loan, passes tax free to the heirs.

The life insurance route is not a one-size-fits-all approach. But when it is appropriate and suitable, it is a wonderful addition to your retirement portfolio.

When you have a mortgage on a home, your first few years of payments are going to interest, not the principal. A permanent life insurance policy works the same way—your first few years of paying premiums are going to the cost of the insurance policy, not the growth of the account value.

The goal is to get as much money into that tax free bucket as possible, knowing you're never going to get all of your money there.

These are incredibly complicated decisions, and there are many factors that determine which options are open to you. And if it wasn't complicated enough, the government rewrites these rules quite often. This is why it's important to work with a professional who can analyze your unique situation and determine which options make the most sense to minimize your tax liability.

This is the reason why I make the investment of my time and finances to be a member of the Elite IRA Advisor group with Ed Slott and Company, LLC. Having access to Ed and his team provides me with current resources to help you with maintaining as much of a tax-efficient retirement income plan as possible.

CHAPTER 9

Social Security, Pensions, and Long-Term Care

When should you turn on Social Security?

To illustrate this, I ask people to imagine three triplets: Stan, Earl, and Del.

Stan turns on Social Security at the standard age—his full retirement age of 67. He wants to get the greatest benefit and doesn't mind waiting until his full retirement age.

Earl turns it on early: age 62. He's run the numbers and thinks, "As long as I live a certain number of years, it will benefit me to take the money early because I don't need it and can invest it."

Del delays turning it on until age 70. He sees that his Social Security benefit will have 8% growth for each year he defers it. Even though his full retirement age is 67, he waits until 70 so he can have the highest possible payout.

So when should you take it? There are so many articles written about this subject every day. Everyone has an opinion on this, but it depends on your unique situation—and your retirement vision.

Do you know your full retirement age? Your full retirement age is determined by your birth date. Once we have that number, analysis comes into play. What will the pros and cons of turning on Social Security early, at full retirement age, or late be for your specific situation?

If your full retirement age is 67, but you're set on retiring at 64, we'll do everything we can to make that work. But if you prioritize getting the highest value out of your Social Security, we'll do everything we can to ensure you make the right decision for your situation.

If we had a crystal ball and knew when you would die, we would know exactly when to turn on Social Security to give you the most value. If you weren't going to live long, it might make sense to take the money early so you can enjoy it while you're living. If you were going to live a long time, we might have you take it late so you get the highest benefit. Since it's impossible to predict the future, all we can do is a thorough analysis to make the best decision.

It's also important to look at the implications of your Social Security decision for the surviving spouse. Remember, when one spouse passes away, the surviving spouse keeps the higher of the two Social Security benefits. So with the loss of the lower benefit, how will you replace that amount of monthly income?

If you're going to do any part time work in retirement, you should not turn on Social Security early. If you take Social Security prior to your full retirement age, you can only earn so much income before your benefits are reduced.

Social Security fills a lot of people with emotion—they get frustrated at the thought of the IRS or the government taking their money. They think the right thing to do is start taking the money at 62 because they're entitled to it. But taking your money early can hurt you in the long run. I encourage everyone to pause, take a breath, and get help with this decision. When you decide when to turn on Social Security, it's irrevocable. You don't want to make this decision from an emotional place.

The Pension Maximalization Formula

The four pension options are:

1) Lump Sum
2) Single Life
3) Life with Period Certain (Spousal Benefit)
4) Joint Life Payout

To determine the best way to leverage your pension, we'll look at the lump sum number and see how it compares with your single life benefit. The single life benefit will last you as long as you have air in your lungs. If you retire and then pass away one week later, that benefit is gone. But if you live another 40 years, it's likely that your total benefit over those years will be higher than the value of the lump sum you could have chosen instead.

Life with period certain comes into play if you have a spouse or adult children that you want to care for or give a legacy to. The "period certain" would usually be 5 or 10 years. The recipient of the pension will receive the pension for their entire lifetime, no matter how long they live. But if they have a 5 year period certain and pass away in year two, their spouse or children will receive the pension for three years. But if the retiree passes away after the five year period, their heirs receive nothing.

A joint life payout reduces the payout even more, but the payout can be the same for the surviving spouse. I don't see this option as often, but people will choose it because they want to ensure their spouse has the exact same amount of income coming in if they should pass away. I had a client who was 15 years older than his wife. Because it was very likely he would pass away years before she did, he wanted to ensure she would be provided for. We selected single life rather than joint life and funded a permanent life insurance policy. The permanent life insurance policy doesn't grow; it's purely a death benefit. Now they can enjoy the highest single life pension payout he can receive for his lifetime. But when he passes away, his surviving spouse receives a tax free sum which can then be converted into lifetime income for her.

You only get one shot at deciding how to take your pension. It's crucial that you get outside advice before you make a choice that could hurt you or your spouse in the long run.

A Different Approach to Long-Term Care

Two out of three people will need some type of long term care in retirement.

Most people come in with the old idea that you need to buy long term care insurance, which can be expensive. But there are other ways to pay for long-term care...

The four options for paying for long term care are:

1) Medicaid
2) Self-insure
3) Insurance
4) Asset-based

If you want to self insure, that's great...but what assets are you going to use? You can't use the assets you're going to use for income to pay for long term care without your income being negatively affected.

With traditional insurance, your rates aren't guaranteed. If the insurance company is behind on claims, they're going to raise your premiums to keep the policy in force. And if you don't ever use it, you lose it. Just because your parents or grandparents had a traditional "use it or lose it" long term care policy, that doesn't mean you have to do that today...

The new approach is to have assets that are specifically set aside for long term care. That way, you can use it if you need it, but if you don't, you can easily leave it to your kids as a tax free death benefit.

The asset-based approach provides the guarantee that either the insured or the beneficiaries will benefit from the money. The rates won't go up, and if you never use it, the funds can pass as a tax-free benefit to your beneficiaries.

If you don't have a plan for long term care, you will put stress on your family. Do you really want to do that to them? Do you want your adult children to put their lives on hold to care for you? When you have a long term care plan, you won't have to worry about placing an unnecessary burden on your family as you age. A long term care plan can allow your family to be care managers instead of care givers.

CHAPTER 10

The Goal – A Retirement Lifestyle You'll Love

The actions you take today will create your ideal retirement tomorrow...

When you take the time to plan your retirement, you're giving yourself the best opportunity to live the retirement you're dreaming of.

Before you made your plan, you didn't know if that dream retirement would be possible.

You've been working for decades, and now you just want to know what day you can retire while being able to afford the lifestyle you want. You don't want to lose the money you've worked for to market volatility.

When I finish making a client's retirement plan, I usually hear, "I wish I'd done this sooner."

The moment that plan is in place, the fear and stress go away.

The unknown is always scarier than reality. Before you make your retirement plan, you can keep yourself up at night imagining all sorts of terrifying worst case scenarios. But when you sit down with a retirement planner, you'll see that those worst case scenarios aren't reality.

Clarity creates peace. When you get that clarity on your retirement, you can let go of all those "what-if" questions stressing you out. You can move from "I don't know when I can retire and if my money will last" to the confidence of having a well-thought-out plan.

The point of retirement planning is to identify your strengths, dangers, and opportunities so we can eliminate the dangers and capture the opportunities by building on your unique strengths.

And the earlier we do this, the easier it is to eliminate any challenges that pop up when we assess your situation.

When we've done that, retirement stops being scary and starts being exciting...

Listen to what my clients had to say about how retirement planning changed their lives:

Caryl L:

"As I was nearing retirement, I was consulting with different financial advisors but was not happy with what I was hearing. Some would tell me I wouldn't be able to retire comfortably with my current investments; others wanted me to take risks that I was not comfortable with and still others were charging fees that were excessive. I knew after those consultations that I needed to work with a financial advisor who was a fiduciary; someone who would look out for my interests.

From our first meeting, I could tell Tim was going to be easy to work with. He laid out all my options and walked me through every detail. Why had no one else explained these options to me?

It has been just over a year since I retired. Even with the current state of the economy, I am able to not worry about what my financial future looks like. I have a limited knowledge of financial investments and I truly feel that Tim gives me the best possible advice and options. I know of others who are very concerned about the losses in their retirement investments. I get to relax and know that because of the work I've done with Tim, I'm in a good place with my financial future."

Rick & Aimee C:

"We both wanted a trusted partner to guide us through the retirement process. Tim was willing to take the time and make us comfortable with and explain the plan we implemented. Other firms we looked at did the minimum or never got back to us at all. As far as our lives now in retirement, we are enjoying a worry-free time, looking forward to our time together, and of course, playing golf."

Matt & Debbie L:

"We had several avenues of retirement savings but not a professional plan. We had tried a couple of planners who we 'thought' had the experience in retirement planning. We found it difficult to find and develop a trustworthy relationship with our previous planners. Those financial planners did not seem to have a credible plan for our future.

Tim's approach to retirement planning was different than all the others we reached out to. He was never high pressure and gave us all the education we needed to make our own decisions.

We now have piece of mind with a solid plan for our future. Through this process we learned not all financial planners specialize in retirement planning and that was the missing piece we were looking for."

Sandy C:

"One of the happiest days of my life was when Tim told me I could retire. When I lost my husband years ago, Tim helped me figure out all the things my husband had neglected to tell me about our finances. My life after retirement has been great. I can't express how wonderful it is to not have to worry. I figure that if there's a problem, Tim will call me. If not, life is good."

John & Penny T:

"Retirement was a huge decision. We both had no idea where we were at financially so we knew we had to try and get some answers. Penny and I just figured we would work till we were old and broke down. Honestly when we reached out to Tim, we were both expecting to have to continue working. Now as we move forward in retirement, it's a relief knowing that Tim has our butts covered. Penny and I are getting along better than ever not having to worry about where we'll be when we really do get old."

Kara J:

"It was very intimidating to think I needed to figure out the path to retirement without guidance, a second set of eyes, and rational thinking. I read and researched many articles on the web regarding planning for a secure financial retirement and I am thankful every day that I decided to call Tim for an appointment. I rest easy today knowing that I have a solid financial plan that will provide financial security for me for my lifetime and a legacy for my daughter in the years to come."

Martha S:

"Retirement was a few years away for me, and as a single lady, I was concerned about what that would look like and if I had enough saved for a long or short life. When I met with Tim, he confirmed that I had saved enough for an annuity that would ensure a steady income for the rest of my life. Six years later, I began receiving my monthly income payments, and I am so thankful that I do not have to worry that I will live longer than my income will last. My monthly income is guaranteed for life."

Each of these clients came to me with worries and fears, but left with the relief and joy of knowing they could afford a retirement they would love. Are you ready to make that transformation?

Disclaimer:

These are unpaid testimonials from current clients. Each client has had a financial relationship with Tim Whisler and is providing their personal opinion. These may present a conflict of interest as one particular client's experience may or may not be the same as another client's experience. Any potential conflict is mitigated by our financial advisor's fiduciary duty to tailor each client's investment objectives to each individual client's own financial situation.

A client testimonial does not guarantee future investment success and should not be indicative that any client or prospective client will experience the same or a higher level of investment performance. Foundations Investment Advisors, LLC is an SEC registered investment adviser. Past performance is not indicative of future results.

Conclusion

If you've read this book to the end, you now know that the #1 thing you can do for yourself to secure your ideal retirement future is to make a plan.

Why wait another day to begin your retirement planning journey or to review your current retirement plan?

The sooner you start, the better advantages and options you'll have. When you start early, your retirement dreams are more likely to come true. Don't deny yourself the benefits of early preparation...

And don't let yourself waste another moment filled with fears, worries, and doubts about your retirement. Don't spend another sleepless night wondering if you'll outlive your money.

When you make your plan, you'll breathe a huge sigh of relief.

You'll have answers to every question that has been plaguing you for years.

You'll have a clear "map" of what your retirement finances will look like.

You'll rest assured that you're financially prepared for any worst-case scenario you can imagine, from a health crisis to the death of a spouse.

You'll have the freedom to retire on your terms.

And now that the scary part is over and your financial well-being is secured, you can sit back, relax, and enjoy your life...

Now, you can make the most of your final working years. You can approach each day at work knowing exactly when you'll retire, and you can turn your focus away from finances to prepare for the professional and emotional transitions that come with retirement.

You can finally get excited about retirement...

You can look forward to your retirement dreams instead of wondering if they'll come true. You can pore over travel websites without fearing that you'll never afford to visit your bucket-list destinations. You can browse beach condo listings without thinking, "Am I being unrealistic?" You can daydream about your retirement plans without a nagging worry that you won't be able to do everything you want to.

Retirement can be the best phase of your life.

With more time and freedom than you've ever had before, this is the phase of life when you get to celebrate all you've accomplished, reap the benefits of your hard work, and make new memories with your loved ones.

But when people haven't made their retirement plans, they forget that...

They think of retirement as something to fear. They let their financial worries form a cloud over the amazing journey they're about to go on.

I don't want anyone to miss out on the joys of retirement because they let fear get the best of them.

If you're ready to leave fear behind and build the future you deserve, I'm here for you.

Next Steps

When you're ready here are three ways we can help you become better prepared for your retirement:

#1. Tune-in to the License to Spend podcast and discover how to avoid taking unnecessary risks in retirement, while finding a greater sense of confidence about your retirement plan. https://whislerwhileyouretire.blubrry.net/

#2. Check your numbers with our easy to use online retirement calculators. Find out if your current retirement savings are enough, what age you should begin saving for retirement, how inflation will impact your retirement income needs, and more.

https://thewhisleragency.com/calculators/

#3. Meet with Tim. Schedule a complimentary consultation to discover how Tim and his team can help you prepare for a stress-free retirement.

https://calendly.com/tim-0491/chat-with-tim

About the Author

Tim Whisler is an experienced financial advisor and founder of The Whisler Agency, an independent financial services firm serving retirees and soon-to-be retirees since 2004. He holds advanced designations as a Chartered Retirement Planning Counselor, Certified for Long-Term Care, and Certified Financial Fiduciary. Tim provides comprehensive retirement income planning services tailored to each client's needs and interests, helping them gain greater confidence in their financial future. He stays current through continuous education and has been featured on major media outlets including Fox Business, Bloomberg, and ABC. Tim also co-authored the book "Protecting Your Assets from Long-Term Care" and hosts the podcast "License to Spend."

He is a member of the Elite IRA Advisor Group with Ed Slott & Company, LLC. Membership in this group requires the completion of requisite training, attending semi-annual workshops, and passing mandatory exams to maintain his position in the group. As an Elite IRA Advisor, Tim helps clients create tax-efficient withdrawal strategies for their retirement income.

On a personal level, Tim and his wife Ronda are both natives of Central Illinois. Together, they're proud parents of their two sons Cam and Cade. They reside in Morton, Illinois along with their adored Boston Terrier, Roxy.

What Clients Are Saying

I met Tim years ago through my parents' trust being made, and from day one I felt like I knew him forever. He was kind, very helpful, explained everything to me very well and no question was ever not answered. I knew someday I was going to inherit what my parents had left for me. Tim is very knowledgeable in his practice and always finds the answer to my questions....I can call him text him at any time of the day or evening and he always responds quickly and in a professional manner.

He has pointed me in the right direction in all of my different investments to help me keep my money safe and I feel he goes over the top sometimes. He will repeat as many times as I need to so I truly understand. I can't thank him enough for taking me under his wing since the loss of both my parents within a year of each other.

– Kelly L.

As I was nearing retirement, I was consulting with different financial advisors but was not happy with what I was hearing. Some would tell me I wouldn't be able to retire comfortably with my current investments; others wanted me to take risks that I was not comfortable with and still others were charging fees that were excessive. I knew after those consultations that I needed to work with a financial advisor who was a fiduciary; someone who would look out for my interests. I actually came across Tim on Facebook. He was offering a webinar and I decided to listen to what he had to say. From that webinar, I could tell he was different (in a good way!). Tim was so informative and I could tell from the start that he would be a good listener. I became hooked on his podcasts. They were so easy to understand and I learned SO MUCH! Although Tim and I are in different states, we have been able to communicate very well via Zoom. From our first meeting, I could tell Tim was going to be easy to work with. He laid out all my options and walked me through every detail. Why had no one else explained these options to me? It has been just over a year since I retired. Even with the current state of the economy, I am able to not worry about what my financial future looks like. I have a limited knowledge of financial investments and I truly feel that Tim gives me the best possible advice and options. I know of others who are very concerned about the losses in their retirement investments. I get to relax and know that because of the work I've done with Tim, I'm in a good place with my financial future.

– Caryl L.

As Harry and I were getting old enough to think about retirement. We saw your ad in the paper, came to your seminar and were immediately drawn to you. The reason being you didn't tell us all the wonderful things you can do for us, you told us how we could work together and you could help us figure out what we wanted to do with our retirement and how we wanted to spend it. We never have regretted that decision. It's one of the best ones we've ever made.

We were also impressed that you don't automatically take everyone. You wanted to meet personally with us to see if we would be a good fit. That makes things very special. You don't have fancy dinners and things like a lot of the places do. You are so genuine and I think that's what drew us to you instantly. We chose you because you are genuine, you've got wonderful plans, you have enthusiasm, and you love what you do for your clients. I've never been disappointed by you ever. I totally and completely trust you. One of the happiest days of my life was when you told me that I could retire, it was just exciting, and you helped me discover so many things after I lost Harry that I didn't know about because he kind of neglected to tell me things. You're always the first one there to get me out of jams, you're not shady in any way, you automatically always welcome my kids, you are totally open, always cheerful. I can't say enough good things about you, I really can't. My life since retirement is great, living the life. Can't tell you how wonderful it is to not have to worry about things because I figure if there's a problem, you'll call me. If there's not, life is good. I trust you totally and completely. I just really am glad that you

came into our lives at the time you did, and I have never regretted
it and I'd be happy to give you recommendations to anyone.

– Sandy C.

We did not have a financial advisor and money in multiple places
and were looking for guidance. You were recommended VERY
highly by our daughter. We knew you were a Christian and
therefore knew you would be a good steward of our money. It is
a comfort knowing we have someone to turn to who can give us
advice, keeps up to date in government and market trends, but
also admits if you don't know the answer to our question.

– John & Vicki G.

No one person can know it all. It is the advisor who recognizes
this fact and subsequently seeks additional knowledge and
professional partnerships that is most successful. Learning is
a commitment, and the payoffs can be exponential. Author Tim
Whisler has pursued his education and admittedly noticed a
higher level of confidence. He confided in me that he has "never
been so equipped, prepared, and empowered as I am at this
moment to be able to confidently advise people on important
topics." That is precisely the type of person we should all want
helping us navigate the financial services industry…while acting
as a watchdog over our finances. And now Tim has published

a book to share his knowledge?!? As an educator myself, this makes me proud.

– Andy Ives, CFP®, AIF®, IRA Analyst,
Ed Slott and Company L.L.C.

We were ready to retire and had been saving, but we did not have a retirement plan nor did we know how to proceed. We had heard Tim's radio advertising over the years and decided to give him a call. Tim returned our call and came for a visit to discuss retirement options. We were under no obligation. Tim gathered background information, asked us what kind of risk level we were comfortable with, and how we wanted to proceed. Tim came back later with different options which we could choose from. We were not pressured to make a decision. As it turned out, we did decide to invest our monies with Tim. Tim is very knowledgeable and continues to improve his skillset for the clients he serves. Tim eases our minds from the stress of investing our monies on our own. Tim has the knowledge of what plans are performing in the industry that are consistent with our risk level. Tim's personality is inviting, like a friend, who we have known for years. When he comes to talk business with us, it does not seem like business. It is more as a friend coming to visit while easing our worries and seeing if anything has changed in our lives to affect our investments. Tim is always available for our questions and a pleasure to work with.

– Mike & Cindy S.

I had a lot of questions about retirement and RMDs and I felt that my former advisor wasn't keeping me informed with my progress toward this milestone in my life.

I attended a webinar of Tim's and had a follow-up meeting with him. From that first meeting, I was immediately impressed with his helpfulness and knowledge. I trusted him from the moment we had that first meeting, and he has never let me down. Whenever I have a question about my finances, Tim is always there. His replies are always timely, and I respect his opinion so much because of my trust in him.

– Debbi L.

Retirement was a huge decision. We both had no idea where we were at financially so we knew we had to try and get some answers. Penny and I just figured we would work till we were old and broke down. Honestly when we reached out to you, we were both expecting to have to continue working. I probably should still be working, but that's another conversation.

When it came time to look for an advisor, we had both talked about reaching out to you. Penny and I always said when it comes time to seek advice financially you were our guy. That we both could remember you from your Farmers insurance days says a lot. You helped us then and stood out as an honest, sincere and down-to-earth guy. We both can remember that! Pretty amazing I think. The fact that you explain everything so well, and that it makes sense in the end is pretty neat for us. You laid out some options and never pushed us, but advised us on what were our best options. When I said you were the man,that was exactly what we both felt.

Now as we move forward in retirement, it's a relief knowing that you have our butts covered. Penny and I are getting along better than ever not having to worry about where we'll be when we really do get old. We always enjoy your visits and can't wait for the book!

– **John & Penny T.**

We looked for a retirement adviser because we knew in a year we would be retiring from teaching and did not have a good clue on how to set up our funds from school, invest new funds, and how to exactly do medicare. We had looked at one other manager but chose not to use him and had some money in another account set up with an investor, but did not feel he was doing the best for us or knew exactly what we were trying to do.

Our son referred you to us. When we learned you were a Christian and would understand most of our thoughts about what to do with our money, we felt we would have a common ground from which to discuss things. We were getting ready to start Medicare, also, and you advised us on how and what to do about that. We felt strongly that we could trust you which probably was at the top of our list of qualities we hoped to have with our adviser and you have proven that to be true.

We have been more than pleased with our relationship with you concerning our finances. You have proven to be on the *same ground as us with our desire to do not just what we can to make money, but with doing it ethically and within a Christian framework. I have enjoyed our subsequent friendship, also. Except for last year when the market hit everyone, we have seen our funds grow and when the market went south, you wisely advised us to move our money out of it. Your recommendation of HealthPartners has been a huge blessing to us as well. We have saved much on prescriptions and on health care. It has been a wonderful thing to see it supply for my wife's current battle with cancer. This year we have met our co-pay already and a grant helped pay the larger part of that, so we are taken care of completely until next year. The new OTC benefit has proven to be very useful and many of our every day needs are met by it. I have appreciated your help in putting the funds my wife inherited from her parents and also helping us put some of our extra money in an account, too.*

– Bill & Carol C.

Prior to working with Tim, my previous financial advisor seemed more interested in multiple churn actions which resulted in additional fees and charges. After some research, I ended up switching to TD Ameritrade where I had more control over the amount of trading and did not incur additional charges.

At the time I was in the process of retiring and my wife and I heard one of Tim's advertisements on the radio which seemed to be in line with where we hoped to be in our financial life.

Since we've been with Tim, I have nothing but respect for his professionalism and guidance and have recommended him to several of our friends. We also appreciate Tim's personality, interest in our needs and desires and his listening ability. Without reading his book ahead of time, I am sure that it will be a worthwhile read and of assistance to future clients in their financial journey.

– Larry & Brenda S.

We wanted to make sure that we were as safe as could be with what we had saved up over the years. And was not sure where we had our investments were doing all that they could. We were referred to you by a family member. Since we've been working with you, we do feel much safer now.

– Bob & Jeri M.

I was not happy with my previous investment advisor. I believe we connected originally with my need for health insurance coverage while I was on staff at Morton Bible Church and I liked how you thought through and guided our journey to cover that. I feel a sense of comfort with our conversations concerning options for my needs at that time.

– Kim & Twila F.

Before working with Tim, we were uncertain of our financial future and uncomfortable with our investments. We heard Tim's radio commercials and thought they were impressive. We were looking for an alternative to the stock market. A mutual friend recommended Tim to us.

Since working with him, we are both more comfortable because we haven't been forced to use our investments.

– Jerry & Katie P.

The Whisler Agency has piloted me through the numerous decisions I've had to make with respect to my retirement planning – secure, solid investments, Medicare, Social Security, and just general future financial planning. It was very intimidating to think I needed to figure out this path without guidance, a second set of eyes, and rational thinking. I read and researched many articles on the web regarding planning for a secure financial retirement and I am thankful every day that I decided to Google for Financial Planners in my area.

I read The Whisler Agency's entire website and decided to call Tim for an appointment. He is always extremely professional, an expert in his field, and a reliable confidante.

I can't praise Tim Whisler and his team enough for everything they have done in these past four and a half years to lend a compassionate and extremely knowledgeable ear to my future financial goals. Tim has provided numerous scenarios to help me make the very important decisions that will become my new financial plan for 2023. I rest easy today knowing that I have a solid financial plan that will provide financial security for me for my lifetime and a legacy for my daughter in the years to come.

Thank you, Tim, and team, for your expert advice, resounding guidance, compassion, and credibility. I would recommend your agency to anyone that feels overwhelmed by the mirage of all things "retirement".

— Kara J.

I heard Tim Whisler's commercial on the radio where he talked about having a guaranteed income for life. He also mentioned not stressing out, day to day, as the market was volatile with its ups and downs. Retirement was a few years away for me, and as a single lady, I was concerned about what that would look like and if I had enough saved for a long or short life. I talked to my best advisor, my father, about Tim's commercial. My father had done a fantastic job with his retirement funds, but he hadn't extended his wisdom to me. My father encouraged me to meet with Tim as soon as possible. When I met with Tim, he confirmed that I had saved enough for an annuity that would ensure a steady income for the rest of my life. I began working with Tim right away. Six years later, I began receiving my monthly income payments, and I am so thankful that I do not have to worry that I will live longer than my income will last. My monthly income is guaranteed for life. Thank you, Tim, for being a joy to work with and making my life easier.

— Martha S.

Cathy and I were going to retire in the very near future. We had both built up fairly decent retirement funds but we didn't know how much to budget, where we needed to transfer our funds to, or how much to withdraw on a monthly basis. Basically, we needed help to manage our investments. We wanted to travel and live a good lifestyle, but not run out of money in the long run.

We had heard Tim's radio commercial and the way he presented himself and his approach to retirement. One thing that really hit home was that he spoke about not losing our retirement savings due to downturns in the stock market. We interviewed Tim and hit it off with him immediately. Other retirement consultants had products that they wanted to "sell" and didn't really propose a program that we needed or wanted. Tim was well-versed in the different options and did not try to force any of them on us. He is very professional. He listened to all our concerns and was very good at answering all our questions. He was very friendly and open. We quickly became friends. Tim helped us move our retirement funds into products that met our goals and are very happy with.

We have been working with Tim for at least 7 years now and are very pleased with everything he has done with us. We can call him anytime about anything and he is very responsive. He is more than willing to come to our house to discuss whatever the concern or question is. Our retirement is going the way we were hoping for and that is due, in part, to our relationship with Tim. We are glad that we heard his radio commercial.

– **Charles & Catherine R.**

I was unhappy with my then-current investment advisor for my retirement portfolio, & wanted a helpful alternative. I chose you because you invested considerable time with me on Zoom call meetings with no requirement that I commit to retaining your services. I felt much more rushed w/ my prior investment advisor - even after I retained him - & during the subsequent single annual in-person review he offered me (I could have demanded more appointments, but didn't as I usually didn't enjoy them). In the course of those numerous no-pressure introductory appointments with you, I felt you understood my objectives, explained processes & products in a language I could understand, and were happy to answer my questions in a way I could understand. I came to feel you were a person I could trust to be an advocate for my comfort level & goals in my personal financial matters. I'm pleased that you proposed the annuity investment vehicle I have in place. Whether or not that was a perfect choice, well, it seemed like a good one for the attention & understanding I was willing to give the process. So, I have some retirement financial peace of mind to a degree as a result. However, economic conditions outside of that decision do give me pause & a degree of angst. I see runaway inflation degrading my buying power, and the cost of Medicare now wiping out the SSA cost of living increase I received this year. I do have the fear that I really don't have much disposable income for leisure pursuits.

– John M.

General Disclaimer

Investment advisory services offered through Foundations Investment Advisors, LLC, an SEC registered investment adviser.

The content in this book reflects the personal opinions, viewpoints and analyses of the author, Tim Whisler, and should not be regarded as a description of advisory services provided by Foundations Investment Advisors, LLC ("Foundations"), or performance returns of any Foundations client.

The views reflected in the commentary are subject to change at any time without notice. Any mention of a particular security and related performance data is not a recommendation to buy or sell that security, or any security. Foundations manages its clients' accounts using a variety of investment techniques and strategies, which are not necessarily discussed in the commentary. Foundations deems reliable any statistical data or information obtained from or prepared by third party sources that is included in any commentary, but in no way guarantees its accuracy or completeness.

Roth Disclaimer

A Roth conversion may not be suitable for your situation. The primary goal in converting retirement assets into a Roth IRA is to reduce the future tax liability on the distributions you take in retirement, or on the distributions of your beneficiaries. The information provided is to help you determine whether or not a Roth IRA conversion may be appropriate for your particular circumstances. Please review your retirement savings, tax, and legacy planning strategies with your legal/tax advisor to be sure a Roth IRA conversion fits into your planning strategies.

Rates and guarantees provided by insurance products and annuities are subject to the financial strength of the issuing insurance company; not guaranteed by any bank or the FDIC.

Client Experience Disclaimer

Comments regarding a particular client's experience may or may not be the same as another client's experience, and is not an indication that any client or prospective client will experience the same or a higher level of future success or performance.

www.ingramcontent.com/pod-product-compliance
Lightning Source LLC
Chambersburg PA
CBHW071603200326
41519CB00021BB/6845